Baby Penguin Slips and Slides

Parent Introduction

This book can be read with children in several different ways. You can read the book to them or, depending on their ability, they may be able to read the book to you. You can also take turns reading! Throughout the book you will find words and phrases in big, bold text. If your child is just beginning to read, you might want to invite your child to participate in reading this text.

Your child may enjoy several readings of this story. With each reading, your child might focus on or see something new. As you read together, consider taking time to discuss the story and the information about the animals. At the end of the story, we have also included some fun questions to talk over together.

Baby Penguin Slips and Slides
A Photo Adventure™ Book

Author	Michael Teitelbaum
Editor	Elizabeth Bennett
Publishing Director	Chester Fisher
Art Director	Sumit Charles
Designers	Joita Das and Rati Mathur
Project Managers	Ravneet Kaur and Shekhar Kapur
Art Editor	Sujatha Menon
Picture Researcher	Shweta Saxena

Picture Credits
t=top b=bottom c=centre l=left r=right m=middle
Front Cover : Juniors Bildarchiv / Photolibrary; Back Cover : Juniors Bildarchiv / Photolibrary; Half Title : DANIEL A BEDELL / Animals Animals / Photolibrary; 3 : Fritz Polking / Photolibrary ; 4 : Tsuneo Nakamura / Volvox Inc / Alamy ; 5 : DAVID MIDDLETON/NHPA ; 6-7 : Juniors Bildarchiv / Photolibrary ; 7 (Inset) : Wayne Tam / Istockphoto ; 8(Inset) :Armin Rose / Shutterstock ; 9 : Bryan & Cherry Alexander Photography / Alamy ; 10 : WorldFoto / Alamy ; 12 : Juniors Bildarchiv / Alamy ; 14 : Elvele Images / Alamy ; 15 : Juniors Bildarchiv / Alamy ; 16 : DAVID TIPLING/ Nature PL ; 17(Inset) : Enrique Aguirre / Oxford Scientific / Photolibrary ; 18(Inset) BRYAN & CHERRY ALEXANDER / NHPA ; 19 : Pete Oxford / Nature PL ; 20-21 : DAVID TIPLING / Nature PL ; 22 : Pete Oxford / Nature PL ; 24 : Juniors Bildarchiv / Alamy

Published by Treasure Bay, Inc.
40 Sir Francis Drake Boulevard
San Anselmo, CA 94960 USA

PRINTED IN SINGAPORE

Library of Congress Catalog Card Number: 2008907572

Hardcover ISBN-10: 1-60115-285-X
Hardcover ISBN-13: 978-1-60115-285-5
Paperback ISBN-10: 1-60115-286-8
Paperback ISBN-13: 978-1-60115-286-2

Visit us online at:
www.TreasureBayPublishing.com

t all the
penguins!

They live on the ice and snow in frozen Antarctica.

3

There is Baby Penguin.

He has **lots** of friends.

They waddle from side to side.

They **run** on the ice.

They even **bump** into each other!

FACT STOP

Father penguins keep the eggs warm, while mother penguins look for food.

5

Baby Penguin and his friends climb up the icy **hill.**

6

Penguins are birds, but they cannot fly.

It takes a long time to get to the **top.**

Now comes the fun part.

Baby Penguin **slides** down the hill on his belly.

Wheeeeee! He lands right next to his dad.

FACT STOP

Some penguins have lived to be 50 years old.

8

Time for hide and seek!

Baby Penguin tries to
hide from his friends.

Can you find him hiding
in the snow?

12

Now it is Baby Penguin's
turn to look for his

friends.

Come out, come out,
wherever you are!

13

Brrr!

Baby Penguin and his friends
are covered with snow.

14

They warm up in the sunshine.

15

16

All that playing has made
Baby Penguin hungry.

Don't worry Baby Penguin.

It is almost time to **eat.**

FACT STOP

Some mother penguins
will walk 50 miles to
the ocean to bring
back food for
their babies.

17

The mother penguin has caught a fish.

She uses her beak to feed some **fish** to Baby Penguin.

FACT STOP

Penguins have webbed feet to help them swim.

18

19

The sunlight is fading away.

Baby Penguin and his friends huddle together to stay **warm** and **snug.**

Good night, Baby Penguin. Sleep tight.

Tomorrow you and your friends can **play** once again.

Look back through the story:

1. Who keeps the penguin eggs warm?

2. What are some things a baby penguin can do with his friends?

3. What can a baby penguin do to stay warm?

4. How would you try to stay warm if you lived in Antarctica?